THE KNOPF POETRY SERIES

The Gold Cell

The Gold Cell

Poems by
Sharon Olds

Alfred A. Knopf   New York   1989

THIS IS A BORZOI BOOK
PUBLISHED BY ALFRED A. KNOPF, INC.

Poems in this work were originally published in the following publications:
*The Agni Review, Alcatraz, The American Poetry Review, The Iowa Review,
Ironwood, Kayak, The Missouri Review, The Nation, The New England
Review, The New Yorker, Open Places, The Paris Review, Poetry East,
Sierra Madre Review, Sonora Review,* and *The Yale Review.*

"Cambridge Elegy," "The Quest," and "The Month of June : 13½" were
originally published in *Poetry.*

Grateful acknowledgment is made to The Monthly Review Foundation for
permission to reprint "Outside the Operating Room of the Sex-Change Doctor,"
by Sharon Olds from *Powers of Desire: The Politics of Sexuality,* edited
by Ann Snitow et al. Copyright © 1983 by Ann Snitow, Christine Stansell, and
Sharon Thompson. Reprinted by permission of The Monthly Review
Foundation.

Library of Congress Cataloging-in-Publication Data

Olds, Sharon.   The gold cell.

  (The Knopf poetry series ; 25)
  I. Title.
PS3565.L34G6 1987   811'.54   86-45511
ISBN 0-394-55699-2
ISBN 0-394-74770-4 (pbk.)

Manufactured in the United States of America
Published January 30, 1987
Reprinted Three Times
Fifth Printing, July 1989

For Ursula Goodenough

Contents

Part Three

Part Four

I

Summer Solstice, New York City

By the end of the longest day of the year he could not stand it,
he went up the iron stairs through the roof of the building
and over the soft, tarry surface
to the edge, put one leg over the complex green tin cornice
and said if they came a step closer that was it.
Then the huge machinery of the earth began to work for his life,
the cops came in their suits blue-grey as the sky on a cloudy evening,
and one put on a bullet-proof vest, a
black shell around his own life,
life of his children's father, in case
the man was armed, and one, slung with a
rope like the sign of his bounden duty,
came up out of a hole in the top of the neighboring building
like the gold hole they say is in the top of the head,
and began to lurk toward the man who wanted to die.
The tallest cop approached him directly,
softly, slowly, talking to him, talking, talking,
while the man's leg hung over the lip of the next world
and the crowd gathered in the street, silent, and the
hairy net with its implacable grid was
unfolded near the curb and spread out and
stretched as the sheet is prepared to receive at a birth.
Then they all came a little closer
where he squatted next to his death, his shirt
glowing its milky glow like something
growing in a dish at night in the dark in a lab and then
everything stopped
as his body jerked and he
stepped down from the parapet and went toward them

3

and they closed on him, I thought they were going to
beat him up, as a mother whose child has been
lost will scream at the child when it's found, they
took him by the arms and held him up and
leaned him against the wall of the chimney and the
tall cop lit a cigarette
in his own mouth, and gave it to him, and
then they all lit cigarettes, and the
red, glowing ends burned like the
tiny campfires we lit at night
back at the beginning of the world.

On the Subway

The boy and I face each other.
His feet are huge, in black sneakers
laced with white in a complex pattern like a
set of intentional scars. We are stuck on
opposite sides of the car, a couple of
molecules stuck in a rod of light
rapidly moving through darkness. He has the
casual cold look of a mugger,
alert under hooded lids. He is wearing
red, like the inside of the body
exposed. I am wearing dark fur, the
whole skin of an animal taken and
used. I look at his raw face,
he looks at my fur coat, and I don't
know if I am in his power—
he could take my coat so easily, my
briefcase, my life—
or if he is in my power, the way I am
living off his life, eating the steak
he does not eat, as if I am taking
the food from his mouth. And he is black
and I am white, and without meaning or
trying to I must profit from his darkness,
the way he absorbs the murderous beams of the
nation's heart, as black cotton
absorbs the heat of the sun and holds it. There is
no way to know how easy this
white skin makes my life, this

life he could take so easily and
break across his knee like a stick the way his
own back is being broken, the
rod of his soul that at birth was dark and
fluid and rich as the heart of a seedling
ready to thrust up into any available light.

The Abandoned Newborn

When they found you, you were not breathing.
It was ten degrees below freezing, and you were
wrapped only in plastic. They lifted you
up out of the litter basket, as one
lifts a baby out of the crib after nap
and they unswaddled you from the Sloan's shopping bag.
As far as you were concerned it was all over,
you were feeling nothing, everything had stopped
some time ago,
and they bent over you and forced the short
knife-blade of breath back
down into your chest, over and
over, until you began to feel
the pain of life again. They took you
from silence and darkness right back
through birth, the gasping, the bright lights, they
achieved their miracle: on the second
day of the new year they brought you
back to being a boy whose parents
left him in a garbage can,
and everyone in the Emergency Room
wept to see your very small body
moving again. I saw you on the news,
the discs of the electrocardiogram
blazing like medals on your body, your hair
thick and ruffed as the head of a weed, your
large intelligent forehead dully
glowing in the hospital TV light, your
mouth pushed out as if you are angry, and

something on your upper lip, a
dried glaze from your nose,
and I thought how you are the most American baby,
child of all of us through your very
American parents, and through the two young medics,
Lee Merklin and Frank Jennings,
who brought you around and gave you their names,
forced you to resume the hard
American task you had laid down so young,
and though I see the broken glass on your path, the
shit, the statistics—you will be a man who
wraps his child in plastic and leaves it in the trash—I
see the light too as you saw it
forced a second time in silver ice between your lids, I am
full of joy to see your new face among us,
Lee Frank Merklin Jennings I am
standing here in dumb American praise for your life.

In the Cell

Sitting in the car at the end of summer, my
feet on the dashboard, the children in the back
laughing, my calf gleaming like a crescent moon,
I notice the hairs are sparser on my legs,
thinning out as I approach middle age—
not like some youth whose vigorous hairs
pulse out of his skin with power while he is
taking a man's genitals off as
slowly as possible, carefully, so as
not to let him get away, to
get all he knows out of him first—
names, locations, human maps of
human cities, in our common tongue and
written with our usual alphabet so he can
rule those maps, change the names of the streets and
line the people along them to turn the
small cells of their faces up to him,
the sun on him like gilding.
This is what I cannot understand, the
innocence of his own body, its
goodness and health, the hairs like sweet
molasses pouring from the follicles of his forearm and
cooling in great looping curls
above the sex of the man he is undoing as
he himself was made.

The Twin

(for Lazarus Colloredo, 17th Century)

He is a large man, with thick hair
and a thick moustache. He holds aside his
cloak, he holds his vest open,
his shirt open. His twin grows
from his chest. Canted over backward toward us
it hangs from him, its arms—jointed like
chicken wings—springing from its ribs and
held with slings, its hands cocked,
the head dangling. Its eyes are closed
and never did open. Its mouth is open
and never did close, and though along the jaws
whiskers appeared, from the mouth there never
came a sound. The luxuriant hair
hangs down from its scalp, nearly touching its
one leg, plump and white, that
dangles on the man's thigh. At birth
they were given one name, but when the man grew up,
his sleeping twin suspended from him with that
slight grin of ecstasy on its
face, floating before him, its skin
his skin, its genitals buried in his body,

he had it baptized, naming the heart
next to his heart. He has placed a lace collar
around the throat swaying in the air,
the half-body that at night curls like a
cat in the curve of his body.
He looks at us, his gaze direct
and without expectation, heavy-lidded eyes
full of weariness, he looks at us
across his brother, the one he named
John the Baptist, who goes before him
into the wilderness.

The Food-Thief

(Uganda, drought)

They drive him along the road in the steady
conscious way they drove their cattle
when they had cattle, when they had homes and
living children. They drive him with pliant
peeled sticks, snapped from trees
whose bark cannot be eaten—snapped,
not cut, no one has a knife, and the trees that can be
eaten have been eaten leaf and trunk and the
long roots pulled from the ground and eaten.
They drive him and beat him, a loose circle of
thin men with sapling sticks,
driving him along slowly, slowly
beating him to death. He turns to them
with all the eloquence of the body, the
wrist turned out and the vein up his forearm
running like a root just under the surface, the
wounds on his head ripe and wet as a
rich furrow cut back and cut back at
plough-time to farrow a trench for the seed, his
eye pleading, the iris black and
gleaming as his skin, the white a dark
occluded white like cloud-cover on the
morning of a day of heavy rain.

His lips are open to his brothers as the body of a
woman might be open, as the earth itself was
split and folded back and wet and
seedy to them once, the lines on his lips
fine as the thousand tributaries of a
root-hair, a river, he is asking them for life
with his whole body, and they are driving his body
all the way down the road because
they know the life he is asking for—
it is their life.

The Girl

They chased her and her friend through the woods
and caught them in a small clearing, broken
random bracken, a couple of old mattresses,
the dry ochre of foam rubber,
as if the place had been prepared.
The thin one with black hair
started raping her best friend,
and the blond one stood above her,
thrust his thumbs back inside her jaws, she was 12,
stuck his penis in her mouth and throat
faster and faster and faster.
Then the black-haired one stood up—
they lay like pulled-up roots at his feet,
two naked 12-year-old girls, he said
Now you're going to know what it's like
to be shot 5 times and slaughtered like a pig,
and they switched mattresses,
the blond was raping and stabbing her friend,
the black-haired one sticking inside her
in one place and then another,
the point of his gun pressed deep into her waist,
she felt a little click in her spine and a
sting like 7-Up in her head and then he
pulled the tree-branch across her throat
and everything went dark,
the gym went dark, and her mother's kitchen,
even the globes of light on the rounded
lips of her mother's nesting bowls went dark.

When she woke up she was lying on the cold
iron-smelling earth, she was under the mattress,

pulled up over her like a
blanket at night,
she saw the body of her best friend
and she began to run,
she came to the edge of the woods and she stepped
out from the trees, like a wound debriding,
she walked across the field to the tracks
and said to the railway brakeman *Please, sir. Please, sir.*

At the trial she had to say everything—
her big sister taught her the words—
she had to sit in the room with them and
point to them. Now she goes to parties
but does not smoke, she is a cheerleader,
she throws her body up in the air
and kicks her legs and comes home and does the dishes
and her homework, she has to work hard in math,
the night over the roof of her bed
filled with white planets. Every night she
prays for the soul of her best friend and
then thanks God for life. She knows
what all of us want never to know
and she does a cartwheel, the splits, she shakes the
shredded pom-poms in her fists.

Outside the Operating Room
of the Sex-Change Doctor

Outside the operating room of the sex-change doctor, a tray of penises.

There is no blood. This is not Vietnam, Chile, Buchenwald. They were surgically removed under anaesthetic. They lie there neatly, each with a small space around it.

The anaesthetic is wearing off now. The chopped-off sexes lie on the silver tray.

One says *I am a weapon thrown down. Let there be no more killing.*

Another says *I am a thumb lost in the threshing machine. Bright straw fills the air. I will never have to work again.*

The third says *I am a caul removed from his eyes. Now he can see.*

The fourth says *I want to be painted by Géricault, a still life with a bust of Apollo, a drape of purple velvet, and a vine of ivy leaves.*

The fifth says *I was a dirty little dog, I knew he'd have me put to sleep.*

The sixth says *I am safe. Now no one can hurt me.*

Only one is unhappy. He lies there weeping in terrible grief, crying out *Father, Father!*

The Solution

Finally they got the Singles problem under control, they made it scientific. They opened huge Sex Centers—you could simply go and state what you want and they would find you someone who wanted that too. You would stand under a sign saying *I Like to Be Touched and Held* and when someone came and stood under the sign saying *I Like to Touch and Hold* they would send the two of you off together.

At first it went great. A steady stream of people under the sign *I Like to Give Pain* paired up with the steady stream of people from under *I Like to Receive Pain. Foreplay Only—No Orgasm* found its adherents, and *Orgasm Only—No Foreplay* matched up its believers. A loyal Berkeley, California, policeman stood under the sign *Married Adults, Lights Out, Face to Face, Under a Sheet,* because that's the only way it was legal in Berkeley—but he stood there a long time in his lonely blue law coat. And the man under *I Like to Be Sung to While Bread Is Kneaded on My Stomach* had been there weeks without a reply.

Things began to get strange. The *Love Only—No Sex* was doing fine; the *Sex Only—No Love* was doing really well, pair after pair walking out together like wooden animals off a child's ark, but the line for *38D or Bigger* was getting unruly, shouting insults at the line for *8 Inches or Longer,* and odd isolated signs were springing up everywhere, *Retired Schoolteacher and Parakeet—No Leather; One Rm/No Bath/View of Sausage Factory.*

The din rose in the vast room. The line under *I Want to Be Fucked Senseless* was so long that portable toilets had to be added and a minister brought in for deaths, births, and marriages on the line. Over under *I Want to Fuck Senseless*—no one, a pile of guns. A hollow roaring filled the enormous gym. More and more people began to move over to *Want to Be Fucked Senseless*. The line snaked around the gym, the stadium, the whole town, out into the fields. More and more people joined it, until *Fucked Senseless* stretched across the nation in a huge wide belt like the Milky Way, and since they had to name it they named it, they called it the American Way.

The Pope's Penis

It hangs deep in his robes, a delicate
clapper at the center of a bell.
It moves when he moves, a ghostly fish in a
halo of silver seaweed, the hair
swaying in the dark and the heat—and at night,
while his eyes sleep, it stands up
in praise of God.

When

I wonder now only when it will happen,
when the young mother will hear the
noise like somebody's pressure cooker
down the block, going off. She'll go out in the yard,
holding her small daughter in her arms,
and there, above the end of the street, in the
air above the line of the trees,
she will see it rising, lifting up
over our horizon, the upper rim of the
gold ball, large as a giant
planet starting to lift up over ours.
She will stand there in the yard holding her daughter,
looking at it rise and glow and blossom and rise,
and the child will open her arms to it,
it will look so beautiful.

II

I Go Back to May 1937

I see them standing at the formal gates of their colleges,
I see my father strolling out
under the ochre sandstone arch, the
red tiles glinting like bent
plates of blood behind his head, I
see my mother with a few light books at her hip
standing at the pillar made of tiny bricks with the
wrought-iron gate still open behind her, its
sword-tips black in the May air,
they are about to graduate, they are about to get married,
they are kids, they are dumb, all they know is they are
innocent, they would never hurt anybody.
I want to go up to them and say Stop,
don't do it—she's the wrong woman,
he's the wrong man, you are going to do things
you cannot imagine you would ever do,
you are going to do bad things to children,
you are going to suffer in ways you never heard of,
you are going to want to die. I want to go
up to them there in the late May sunlight and say it,
her hungry pretty blank face turning to me,
her pitiful beautiful untouched body,
his arrogant handsome blind face turning to me,
his pitiful beautiful untouched body,
but I don't do it. I want to live. I
take them up like the male and female
paper dolls and bang them together
at the hips like chips of flint as if to
strike sparks from them, I say
Do what you are going to do, and I will tell about it.

Saturn

He lay on the couch night after night,
mouth open, the darkness of the room
filling his mouth, and no one knew
my father was eating his children. He seemed to
rest so quietly, vast body
inert on the sofa, big hand
fallen away from the glass.
What could be more passive than a man
passed out every night—and yet as he lay
on his back, snoring, our lives slowly
disappeared down the hole of his life.
My brother's arm went in up to the shoulder
and he bit it off, and sucked at the wound
as one sucks at the sockets of lobster. He took
my brother's head between his lips
and snapped it like a cherry off the stem. You would have seen
only a large, handsome man
heavily asleep, unconscious. And yet
somewhere in his head his soil-colored eyes
were open, the circles of the whites glittering
as he crunched the torso of his child between his jaws,
crushed the bones like the soft shells of crabs
and the delicacies of the genitals
rolled back along his tongue. In the nerves of his gums and
bowels he knew what he was doing and he could not
stop himself, like orgasm, his
boy's feet crackling like two raw fish
between his teeth. This is what he wanted,
to take that life into his mouth
and show what a man could do—show his son
what a man's life was.

What if God

And what if God had been watching when my mother
came into my bed? What would He have done when her
long adult body rolled on me like a
tongue of lava from the top of the mountain and the
tears jumped from her ducts like hot rocks and my
bed shook with the tremors of the magma and the
deep cracking of my nature across—
what was He? Was He a bison to lower his
thundercloud head and suck His own sex while He
watched us weep and pray to Him or
was He a squirrel, reaching down through the
hole she broke in my shell, squirrel with His
arm in the yolk of my soul up to the elbow,
stirring, stirring the gold? Or was He a
kid in Biology, dissecting me while she
held my split carapace apart so He could
firk out my oblong eggs one by one, was He a
man entering me up to the hilt while she
pried my thighs wide in the starry dark—
she said that all we did was done in His sight so
what was He doing as He saw her weep in my
hair and slip my soul from between my
ribs like a tiny hotel soap, did He
wash His hands of me as I washed my
hands of Him? Is there a God in the house?
Is there a God in the house? Then reach down and
take that woman off that child's body,
take that woman by the nape of the neck like a young cat and
lift her up and deliver her over to me.

History: 13

When I found my father that night, the blood
smeared on his head and face, I did not
know who had done it. I had loved his body
whole, his head, his face, untouched,
and now he floated on the couch, his arms
up, like Mussolini hanging
upside down in the air, his head
dangling where they could reach him with boards and their
fingernails, those who had lived
under his tyranny.
I saw how the inside of the body could be
brought to the surface, to cover the skin,
his heart standing on his face, the weight of his
body pressing down on his head,
his life slung in the bag of his scalp,
and who had done it? Had I, had my mother,
my brother, my sister, we who had been silent
under him, under him for years? He lay in his
gore all night, as the body hung all
day outside the gas station in
Milan, and when they helped him up and
washed him and he left, I did not see it—
I was not there for the ashes, I had been there
only for the fire, I had seen my father
strung and mottled, mauled as if taken and
raked by a crowd, and I of the crowd
over his body, and how could the day be
good after that, how could anything be good
in such a world, I turned my back
on happiness, at 13 I entered
a life of mourning, of mourning for the Fascist.

26

The Meal

Mama, I never stop seeing you there
at the breakfast table when I'd come home from school—
sitting with your excellent skeletal posture
facing that plate with the one scoop of cottage cheese on it,
forcing yourself to eat, though you did not want to live,
feeding yourself, small spoonful by
small spoonful, so you would not die and
leave us without a mother as you were
left without a mother. You'd sit
in front of that mound rounded as a breast and
giving off a cold moony light,
light of the life you did not want, you would
hold yourself there and stare down at it,
an orphan forty years old staring at the breast,
a freshly divorced woman down to 82 pounds
staring at the cock runny with milk gone sour,
a daughter who had always said
the best thing her mother ever did for her
was to die. I came home every day to
find you there, dry-eyed, unbent, that
hot control in the breakfast nook, your
delicate savage bones over the cheese
curdled like the breast of the mother twenty years in the
porous earth,
            and yet what I remember is your
spoon moving like the cock moving in the
body of the girl waking to the power of her pleasure,
your spoon rising in courage, bite after bite, you
tilted rigid over that plate until you
polished it for my life.

Alcatraz

When I was a girl, I knew I was a man
because they might send me to Alcatraz
and only men went to Alcatraz.
Every time we drove to the city I'd
see it there, white as a white
shark in the shark-rich Bay, the bars like
milk-white ribs. I knew I had pushed my
parents too far, my inner badness had
spread like ink and taken me over, I could
not control my terrible thoughts,
terrible looks, and they had often said
they would send me there—maybe the very next
time I spilled my milk, *Ala
Cazam*, the iron doors would slam, I'd be
there where I belonged, a girl-faced man in the
prison no one had escaped from. I did not
fear the other prisoners,
I knew who they were, men like me who had
spilled their milk one time too many,
not been able to curb their thoughts—
what I feared was the horror of the circles: circle of
sky around the earth, circle of
land around the Bay, circle of
water around the island, circle of
sharks around the shore, circle of
outer walls, inner walls,
iron girders, steel bars,
circle of my cell around me, and there at the
center, the glass of milk and the guard's
eyes upon me as I reached out for it.

San Francisco

When we'd go to San Francisco, my father would
seek out the steepest streets
despite my begging, offering him
a month's allowance—he would sit behind the
wheel and laugh with love, his face
red as a lobster at Fisherman's Wharf
after they drop it green and waving into
boiling water. His black eyes would
snap like seeds popping from a pod,
his black hair would smoke in that salty
air, he would tilt the huge nose of our
car up and press on the gas, he
would not look at me. We'd begin
the ascent, nearly vertical,
tires about to lose their grip on those
slanted cobbles, he'd inch us up, like an
engineering experiment
we'd barely rise, till we hung in space from
nothing, like driving up an elevator shaft,
the black pull of the earth's weight
sucking us back, he'd slow down more and
more, we'd barely rise past buildings
pressed to the side of the precipice like
trees up the face of a cliff. As we neared the
top he went slower and slower and then
shifted into first, trying not to smile,
and in that silence between gears
I would break, weeping and peeing, the fluids of my
body bursting out like people from the
windows of a burning high-rise.
We'd hit the peak, tilt level

and I wouldn't care, what was life when the
man who had made my body liked to
dangle it over empty space and
tease me with death. He sat there sparkling, a
refuse dump, I could smell his heat,
the wheel loose in his hands now, the
reins of my life held slack.
We'd climb out, my knees shaking and I
stank, to look at the world spread out at our
feet as if we owned it,
as if we had power over our lives,
as if my father had control of himself
or I of my fate—
                    far below us,
blue and dazzling, the merciless cold
beauty of the Bay, my whole saved life ahead of me.

Looking at My Father

I do not think I am deceived about him.
I know about the drinking, I know he's a tease,
obsessive, rigid, selfish, sentimental,
but I could look at my father all day
and not get enough: the large creased
ball of his forehead, slightly aglitter like the
sheen on a well-oiled baseball glove;
his eyebrows, the hairs two inches long,
black and silver, reaching out in
continual hope and curtailment; and most of
all I could look forever at his eyes,
the way they bulge out as if eager to see and
yet are glazed as if blind, the whites
hard and stained as boiled eggs
boiled in sulphur water, the irises
muddy as the lip of a live volcano, the
pupils glittering pure black,
magician black. Then there is his nose
rounded and pocked and comfy as the bulb of a
horn a clown would toot, and his lips
solid and springy. I even like to
look in his mouth, stained brown with
cigars and bourbon, my eyes sliding down the
long amber roots of his teeth,
right in there where Mother hated, and
up the scorched satin of the sides and
vault, even the knobs on the back of his
tongue. I know he is not perfect but my
body thinks his body is perfect, the

fine stretched coarse pink
skin, the big size of him, the
sour-ball mass, darkness, hair,
sex, legs even longer than mine,
lovely feet. What I know I know, what my
body knows it knows, it likes to
slip the leash of my mind and go and
look at him, like an animal
looking at water, then going to it and
drinking until it has had its fill and can
lie down and sleep.

Why My Mother Made Me

Maybe I am what she always wanted,
my father as a woman,
maybe I am what she wanted to be
when she first saw him, tall and smart,
standing there in the college yard with the
hard male light of 1937
shining on his black hair. She wanted that
power. She wanted that size. She pulled and
pulled through him as if he were dark
bourbon taffy, she pulled and pulled and
pulled through his body until she drew me out,
rubbery and gleaming, her life after her life.
Maybe I am the way I am
because she wanted exactly that,
wanted there to be a woman
a lot like her, but who would not hold back, so she
pressed herself hard against him,
pressed and pressed the clear soft
ball of herself like a stick of beaten cream
against his stained sour steel grater
until I came out the other side of his body,
a big woman, stained, sour, sharp,
but with that milk at the center of my nature.
I lie here now as I once lay
in the crook of her arm, her creature,
and I feel her looking down into me the way the
maker of a sword gazes at his face in the
steel of the blade.

Now I Lay Me

It is a fine prayer, it is an excellent prayer, really,
Now I lay me down to sleep—
the immediacy, and the power of the child
taking herself up in her arms
and laying herself down on her bed
as if she were her own mother,
Now I lay me down to sleep,
I pray the Lord my soul to keep,
her hands knotted together knuckle by knuckle,
feeling her heart beating in the knuckles,
that heart that did not belong to her yet
that heart that was just the red soft string in her
chest that they plucked at will.
Knees on the fine dark hair-like hardwood
beams of the floor—the hairs of a huge animal—
she commended herself to the care of some reliable keeper
above her parents, someone who had a
cupboard to put her soul in for the night,
one they had no key to, out of their reach
so they could not crack it with an axe, so that
all night there was a part of her
they could not touch. Unless when God had it
she did not have it, but lay there a raw
soulless animal for them to do their dirt on—
coming toward her room with those noises at night and their
fur and their thick varnished hairs.
If I should die before I wake seemed so
possible, so likely really,
the father with the blood on his face,
the mother down to 82 pounds, it was a
mark of doom and a benison

to be able to say *I pray the Lord
my soul to take*—the chance that, dead,
she'd be safe for eternity, which was so much
longer than those bad nights—
she herself could see each morning the
blessing of the white dawn, like some true god coming,
she could get up and wade in the false
goodness of another day.
It was all fine except for the word *take*,
that word with the claw near the end of it.
What if the Lord were just another one of those takers
like her mother, what if the Lord were no bigger than her father,
what if each night those noises she heard
were not her mother and father struggling to
do it or not do it, what if those
noises were the sound of the Lord wrestling with her father
on the round white bedroom rug,
fighting over her soul, and what if the
Lord, who did not eat real food,
got weaker, and her father with all he ate and
drank got stronger, what if the Lord
lost? *God bless Mommy and Daddy and
Trisha and Dougie and Gramma Hester and
Grampa Harry in Heaven*, and then the
light went out, the last of the terrible kisses,
and then she was alone in the dark
and the darkness started to grow there in her room
as it liked to do, and then the night began.

The Chute

When I was a kid, my father built a
hole down through the center of the house.
It started in the upstairs closet, a
black, square mouth like a well
with a lid on it, it plummeted down
behind the kitchen wall, and the raw
pine cloaca tip of it was
down in the basement where the twisted wicker
basket lay on the cement floor,
so when someone dropped in laundry at the top, it would
drop with the speed of sheer falling—in the
kitchen you'd hear that whisk of pure
descent behind the wall. And halfway
down there was an electric fixture for the
doorbell—that bell my father would ring and
ring years later when he stood at the door with that
blood on him, like a newborn's caul,
ringing ringing to enter. But back
then he was only halfway down, a
wad of sheets stuck in the chute,
he could still fix the doorbell when it busted.
He'd stand his kids in front of him,
three skinny scared braggart kids,
and run his gaze over them, a
surgeon running his eyes over the tray,
and he'd select a kid, and take that kid by the
ankles and slowly feed that kid
down the chute. First you'd do a handstand on the
lip of it and then he'd lower you in,
the smell of pine and dirty laundry,

his grip on your ankles like the steel he sold,
he'd lower you until your whole body was in it
and you'd find the little wires, red and
blue, like a vein and a nerve, and you'd tape them together.
We thought it was such an honor to be chosen,
and like all honors it was mostly terror, not
only the blood in your head like a sac of
worms in wet soil, but how could you believe he would
not let go? He would joke about it,
standing there, holding his kid like a
bottle brush inside a bottle, or the
way they drown people, he'd lower us down as if
dipping us into the darkness before birth
and he'd pretend to let go—he loved to hear
passionate screaming in a narrow space—
how could you trust him? And then if you were
his, half him, your left hand maybe and your
left foot dipped in the gleaming
murky liquor of his nature, how could you
trust yourself? What would it feel like
to be on the side of life? How did the
good know they were good, could they look at their
hand and see, under the skin, the
greenish light? We hung there in the dark
and yet, you know, he never dropped us
or meant to, he only liked to say he would,
so although it's a story with some cruelty in it,
finally it's a story of love
and release, the way the father pulls you out of nothing
and stands there foolishly grinning.

The Blue Dress

The first November after the divorce
there was a box from my father on my birthday—no card, but a
big box from Hink's, the dark
department store with a balcony and
mahogany rail around the balcony, you could
stand and press your forehead against it
until you could almost feel the dense
grain of the wood, and stare down
into the rows and rows of camisoles,
petticoats, bras, as if looking down
into the lives of women. The box
was from there, he had braved that place for me
the way he had entered my mother once
to get me out. I opened the box—I had
never had a present from him—
and there was a blue shirtwaist dress
blue as the side of a blue teal
disguised to go in safety on the steel-blue water.
I put it on, a perfect fit,
I liked that it was not too sexy, just a
blue dress for a 14-year-old daughter the way
Clark Kent's suit was just a plain suit for a reporter, but I

felt the weave of that mercerized Indian Head cotton
against the skin of my upper arms and my
wide thin back and especially the skin of my
ribs under those new breasts I had
raised in the night like earthworks in commemoration of his name.
A year later, during a fight about
just how awful my father had been,
my mother said he had not picked out the dress,
just told her to get something not too expensive, and then
had not even sent a check for it,
that's the kind of man he was. So I
never wore it again in her sight
but when I went away to boarding school I
wore it all the time there,
loving the feel of it, just
casually mentioning sometimes it was a gift from my father,
wanting in those days to appear to have something
whether it was true or a lie, I didn't care, just to
have something.

Late Poem to My Father

Suddenly I thought of you
as a child in that house, the unlit rooms
and the hot fireplace with the man in front of it,
silent. You moved through the heavy air
in your physical beauty, a boy of seven,
helpless, smart, there were things the man
did near you, and he was your father,
the mold by which you were made. Down in the
cellar, the barrels of sweet apples,
picked at their peak from the tree, rotted and
rotted, and past the cellar door
the creek ran and ran, and something was
not given to you, or something was
taken from you that you were born with, so that
even at 30 and 40 you set the
oily medicine to your lips
every night, the poison to help you
drop down unconscious. I always thought the
point was what you did to us
as a grown man, but then I remembered that
child being formed in front of the fire, the
tiny bones inside his soul
twisted in greenstick fractures, the small
tendons that hold the heart in place
snapped. And what they did to you
you did not do to me. When I love you now,
I like to think I am giving my love
directly to that boy in the fiery room,
as if it could reach him in time.

June 24

(for my father)

I look at the date, and it has such a look of
fullness, the fat juicy word June and then the
2 and the 4, like a couple and a couple coupled,
the whole date such a look of satiety and plenitude,
and then I remember today is your birthday,
you are 68, it is the birthday of an aging man
and yet I feel such celebration,
as if you were newborn. And it's not just the
turgid redness of your face, or your plump
fleshy hands, appealing as a baby's,
it isn't your earth-brown physical eyes
blank as a baby's lacking knowledge and memory,
it isn't just that a man of 68
is young still, you could have a child
after my own fertility is gone,
a baby dark and smart as you were
the hour of your birth, when your skin shone with the
oil of the world that lies on either
side of our world. The day moves me
because you were given back to me.
You died night after night in the years of my childhood,
sinking down into speechless torpor,
and then you were told to leave for good
and you left, for better, for worse, for a long
time I did not see you or touch you—
and then, as if to disprove the ascendancy of darkness,

little by little you came back to me
until now I have you, a living father
standing in the California sun
unwrapping the crackling caul off a cigar
and placing it in the center of his mouth
where the parent is placed, at the center of the child's life.

After 37 Years My Mother
Apologizes for My Childhood

When you tilted toward me, arms out
like someone trying to walk through a fire,
when you swayed toward me, crying out you were
sorry for what you had done to me, your
eyes filling with terrible liquid like
balls of mercury from a broken thermometer
skidding on the floor, when you quietly screamed
Where else could I turn? Who else did I have?, the
chopped crockery of your hands swinging toward me, the
water cracking from your eyes like moisture from
stones under heavy pressure, I could not
see what I would do with the rest of my life.
The sky seemed to be splintering like a window
someone is bursting into or out of, your
tiny face glittered as if with
shattered crystal, with true regret, the
regret of the body. I could not see what my
days would be with you sorry, with
you wishing you had not done it, the
sky falling around me, its shards
glistening in my eyes, your old soft
body fallen against me in horror I
took you in my arms, I said *It's all right,
don't cry, it's all right*, the air filled with
flying glass, I hardly knew what I
said or who I would be now that I had forgiven you.

201 Upper Terrace, San Francisco

We were up and down the sickening hills of the city
and then at the top, at the tip, I saw
the sign, the street where I had lived as a baby. We drove
up it and up it till three streets
fell away as if plummeting and I
recognized it, a small building with
naked picture windows—the shape of those
rectangles burned on my 3-year-old mind—we
stopped for a moment by the front archway, a
hole in the building like the gates of birth,
dark and tiled inside, dark
spiked plants. I gazed on it as you'd
gaze on a cell where you had been kept, with
awe and terror, I realized
I was conceived here, at the top of this white
hill with the three streets sliding down
straight as water, these two blind rectangle
eyes facing this Western bay as she
stood at the window afterwards and I
whipped my tail and sailed up and
saw the egg like a trap door in the
side of the jail and I pushed through it
head first, my tail fell off I be-
gan to explode in ecstasy re-
leased, released, and in nine months they
lifted me up to the view and said to me
This is the world we give you, and said to the
view, We give you this girl.

44

III

California Swimming Pool

On the dirt, the dead live-oak leaves
lay like dried-out turtle shells,
scorched and crisp, their points sharp as
wasps' stingers. Sated mosquitoes
hung in the air like sharks in water,
and when you held up a tuna sandwich
a gold sphere of yellow-jackets
formed around your hand in the air
and moved when you moved. Everything circled
around the great pool, blue and
glittering as the sacred waters at
Crocodilopolis, and the boys
came from underwater like that
to pull you down. But the true center was the
dressing rooms: the wet suits,
the smell of chlorine, cold concrete,
the splintered pine wall, on the other
side of which were boys, actually
naked there in air clouded as the
shadows at the bottom of the pool, where the crocodiles
glistened in their slick skins. All summer
the knothole in the wall hissed at me
come see, come see, come eat and be eaten.

First Boyfriend

(for D.R.)

We would park on any quiet street,
gliding over to the curb as if by accident,
the houses dark, the families sealed into them,
we'd park away from the street-light, just the
faint waves of its amber grit
reached your car, you'd switch off the motor and
turn and reach for me, and I would
slide into your arms as if I had been born for it,
the ochre corduroy of your sports jacket
pressing the inside of my wrist,
making its pattern of rivulets,
water rippling out like sound waves from a source.
Your front seat had an overpowering
male smell, as if the chrome had been
rubbed with jism, a sharp stale
delirious odor like the sour plated
taste of the patina on an old watch, the
fragrance of your sex polished till it shone in the night, the
jewel of Channing Street, of Benvenue Avenue, of
Panoramic, of Dwight Way, I
returned to you as if to the breast of my father,

grain of the beard on your umber cheeks,
delicate line of tartar on the edge of your teeth,
the odor of use, the stained brass
air in the car as if I had come
back to a pawnshop to claim what was mine—
and as your tongue went down my throat,
right down the central nerve of my body, the
gilt balls of the street-light gleamed like a
pawnbroker's over your second-hand Chevy and
all the toasters popped up and
all the saxophones began to play
hot riffs of scat for the return of their rightful owners.

First Sex

(for J.)

I knew little, and what I knew
I did not believe—they had lied to me
so many times, so I just took it as it
came, his naked body on the sheet,
the tiny hairs curling on his legs like
fine, gold shells, his sex
harder and harder under my palm
and yet not hard as a rock his face cocked
back as if in terror, the sweat
jumping out of his pores like sudden
trails from the tiny snails when his knees
locked with little clicks and under my
hand he gathered and shook and the actual
flood like milk came out of his body, I
saw it glow on his belly, all they had
said and more, I rubbed it into my
hands like lotion, I signed on for the duration.

First Love

(for Averell)

It was Sunday morning, I had *The New York*
Times spread out on my dormitory floor, its
black print coming off dark silver on the
heels of my palms, it was spring and I had the
dormer window of my room open, to
let it in, I even had the radio
on, I was letting it all in, the
tiny silvery radio voices—I
even let myself feel that it was Easter, the
dark flower of his life opening
again, his life being given back
again, I was in love and I could take it, the ink
staining my hands, the news on the radio
coming in my ears, there had been a wreck
and they said your name, son of the well-known they
said your name. Then they said where they'd
taken the wounded and the dead, and I called the
hospital, I remember kneeling by the
phone on the third-floor landing of the dorm, the
dark steep stairs down
next to me, I spoke to a young
man a young doctor there in the
Emergency Room, my open ear
pressed to the dark receiver, my open
life pressed to the world, I said
Which one of them died, and he said your name,
he was standing there in the room with you
saying your name.
              I remember I leaned my

forehead against the varnished bars of the
baluster rails and held on,
pulling at the rails as if I wanted to
pull them together, shut them like a dark
door, close myself like a door
as you had been shut, closed off, but I could not
do it, the pain kept coursing through me like
life, like the gift of life.

Cambridge Elegy

(for Henry Averell Gerry, 1941–60)

I hardly know how to speak to you now,
you are so young now, closer to my daughter's age
than mine—but I have been there and seen it, and must
tell you, as the seeing and hearing
spell the world into the deaf-mute's hand.
The tiny dormer windows like the ears of a fox, like the
long row of teats on a pig, still
perk up over the Square, though they're digging up the
street now, as if digging a grave,
the shovels shrieking on stone like your car
sliding along on its roof after the crash.
How I wanted everyone to die if you had to die,
how sealed into my own world I was,
deaf and blind. What can I tell you now,
now that I know so much and you are a
freshman still, drinking a quart of orange juice and
playing three sets of tennis to cure a hangover, such an
ardent student of the grown-ups! I can tell you
we were right, our bodies were right, life was
really going to be that good, that
pleasurable in every cell.
Suddenly I remember the exact look of your body, but
better than the bright corners of your eyes, or the
light of your face, the rich Long Island
puppy-fat of your thighs, or the slick
chino of your pants bright in the corners of my eyes, I
remember your extraordinary act of courage in
loving me, something no one but the
blind and halt had done before. You were
fearless, you could drive after a sleepless night

just like a grown-up, and not be afraid, you could
fall asleep at the wheel easily and
never know it, each blond hair of your head—and they were
thickly laid—put out like a filament of light,
twenty years ago. The Charles still
slides by with that ease that made me bitter when I
wanted all things hard as your death was hard;
wanted all things broken and rigid as the
bricks in the sidewalk or your love for me
stopped cell by cell in your young body.
Ave—I went ahead and had the children,
the life of ease and faithfulness, the
palm and the breast, every millimeter of delight in the body,
I took the road we stood on at the start together, I
took it all without you as if
in taking it after all I could most
honor you.

Still Life

I lie on my back after making love,
breasts white in shallow curves like the lids of soup dishes,
nipples shiny as berries, speckled and immutable.
My legs lie down there somewhere in the bed like those
great silver fish drooping over the edge of the table.
Scene of destruction, scene of perfect peace,
sex bright and calm and luminous as the
scarlet and blue dead pheasant all
maroon neck feathers and deep body wounds,
and on the center of my forehead a drop of water
round and opalescent, and in it
the self-portrait of the artist, upside down,
naked, holding your brushes dripping like torches with light.

Greed and Aggression

Someone in Quaker meeting talks about greed and aggression
and I think of the way I lay the massive
weight of my body down on you
like a tiger lying down in gluttony and pleasure on the
elegant heavy body of the eland it eats,
the spiral horn pointing to the sky like heaven.
Ecstasy has been given to the tiger,
forced into its nature the way the
forcemeat is cranked down the throat of the held goose,
it cannot help it, hunger and the glory of
eating packed at the center of each
tiger cell, for the life of the tiger and the
making of new tigers, so there will
always be tigers on the earth, their stripes like
stripes of night and stripes of fire-light—
so if they had a God it would be striped,
burnt-gold and black, the way if
I had a God it would renew itself the
way you live and live while I take you as if
consuming you while you take me as if
consuming me, it would be a God of
love as complete satiety,
greed and fullness, aggression and fullness, the
way we once drank at the body of an animal
until we were so happy we could only
faint, our mouths running, into sleep.

It

Sometimes we fit together like the creamy
speckled three-section body of the banana, that
joke fruit, as sex was a joke when we were kids,
and sometimes it is like a jagged blue comb of glass across
my skin,
and sometimes you have me bent over as thick paper can be
folded, on the rug in the center of the room
far from the soft bed, my knuckles
pressed against the grit in the grain of the rug's
braiding where they
laid the rags tight and sewed them together,
my ass in the air like a lily with a wound on it
and I feel you going down into me as
if my own tongue is your cock sticking
out of my mouth like a stamen, the making and
breaking of the world at the same moment,
and sometimes it is sweet as the children we had
thought were dead being brought to the shore in the
narrow boats, boatload after boatload.
Always I am stunned to remember it,
as if I have been to Saturn or the bottom of a trench in the
sea floor, I
sit on my bed the next day with my mouth open and think of it.

57

Topography

After we flew across the country we
got in bed, laid our bodies
delicately together, like maps laid
face to face, East to West, my
San Francisco against your New York, your
Fire Island against my Sonoma, my
New Orleans deep in your Texas, your Idaho
bright on my Great Lakes, my Kansas
burning against your Kansas your Kansas
burning against my Kansas, your Eastern
Standard Time pressing into my
Pacific Time, my Mountain Time
beating against your Central Time, your
sun rising swiftly from the right my
sun rising swiftly from the left your
moon rising slowly from the left my
moon rising slowly from the right until
all four bodies of the sky
burn above us, sealing us together,
all our cities twin cities,
all our states united, one
nation, indivisible, with liberty and justice for all.

A Woman in Heat Wiping Herself

High in the inner regions of my body
this gloss is spun, high up
under the overhanging ledge where the
light pours down on the cliff night and day.
No workers stand around in the
camaraderie of workers,
no one lays the color down on the
lip of the braid, there is only the light,
bands and folds of light, and the clean
sand at the edge, the working surface—there is
no one around for miles, no one hungry,
no one being fed. Just as in the side of the
lamb no one is tending the hole where the
light pours out, no one is folding or
carding while the gold grease of the floss
flows through the follicle, beading and rippling back and
curving forward in solemn spillage.
Things done with no reference to the human.
Most things are done with no reference to the human
even if they happen inside us, in our
body that is far beyond our powers, that we could
never invent. Deep in my sex, the
glittering threads are thrown outward and thrown outward
the way the sea lifts up the whole edge of its body,
the rim, the slit where once or twice in a lifetime
you can look through and see the other world—
it is this world, without us,
this earth and our bodies
without us watching.

The Premonition

When we got to the island, I would drive the kids
over to the Community Center,
its parking lot seething with children, a
spawn of faces in the rear-view mirror,
tops of heads just visible
over the trunk of the car.
I was so afraid I'd run over a child
I had to park somewhere else, I
felt the car straining forward,
lunging like a hungry shark.
I could see the still arms, the scarlet
herringbone pattern across a chest, the
head cracked like a smooth brown egg—I
saw it so clearly I thought it was a warning, I went
slower and slower, wild to be careful,
feeling safe only at home,
in bed, your body an ivory tower
inside my body, and then the condom
ripped and the seed tore into me like a
flame tearing out the top of a tower
into the night, you said you didn't
want another child at all,
and then I knew who it was, the one in the
center of the pool of blood, the dark
marks of the tread all over its chest where the
car had been driven over it back and forth, back and forth.

I Cannot Forget the Woman
in the Mirror

Backwards and upside down in the twilight, that
woman on all fours, her head
dangling and suffused, her lean
haunches, the area of darkness, the flanks and
ass narrow and pale as a deer's and those
breasts hanging down toward the center of the earth
                          like plummets, when I
swayed from side to side they swayed, it was
so dark I couldn't tell if they were gold or
plum or rose. I cannot get over her
moving toward him upside down in the mirror like a
fly on the ceiling, her head hanging down and her
tongue long and black as an anteater's
going toward his body, she was so clearly an
animal, she was an Iroquois scout creeping
naked and noiseless, and when I looked at her
she looked at me so directly, her eyes so
dark, her stare said to me I
belong here, this is mine, I am living out my
true life on this earth.

Love in Blood Time

When I saw my blood on your leg, the drops so
dark and clear, that real arterial red,
I could not even think about death, you
stood there smiling at me,
you squatted in the tub on your long haunches
and washed it away.
The large hard bud of your sex in my mouth,
the dark petals of my sex in your mouth,
I could feel death going farther and farther away,
forgetting me, losing my address, his
palm forgetting the curve of my cheek in his hand.
Then when we lay in the small glow of the
lamp and I saw your lower lip
glazed with light like liquid fire
I looked at you and I tell you I knew you were God
and I was God and we lay in our bed
on the dark cloud, and somewhere down there
was the earth, and somehow all we did, the
blood, the pink stippling of the head, the
pearl fluid out of the slit, the
goodness of all we did would somehow get
down there, it would find its flowering in the world.

This

Maybe if I did not have this
I would call myself my mother's daughter
or identify my soul with the blue bowl
that stood on the table, or with the gold wall, or the field.
I would call myself Cobb, Stuart, Torrance,
McLean, I would wear the plaid at all times,
clan green, blood red,
fine line of the purple vein,
if I did not have this. Or I would wrap my life in the
flag, in its wide swaths of blood, its
stars like broken bowls on that table,
or the cupped curve of my father's cereal-bowl forehead
here above my brows, or my mother's bad vein
running up the inside of my leg
like a river under the land.
                                    But I have this,
so this is who I am, this body
white as yellowish dough brushed with dry flour
pressed to his body. I am these breasts that
crush against him like collapsible silver
travel cups that telescope into themselves,
and the nipples that float in the center like hard
raspberries in bright sunlight, they
are my life, the dark sex that
takes him in as anyone in summer will
open their throat to the hose held up
hot on the edge of the sandlot—don't
ask me about my country or who my
father was or even what I do, if you
want to know who I am, I am this, *this*.

IV

The Moment the Two Worlds Meet

That's the moment I always think of—when the
slick, whole body comes out of me,
when they pull it out, not pull it but steady it
as it pushes forth, not catch it but keep their
hands under it as it pulses out,
they are the first to touch it,
and it shines, it glistens with the thick liquid on it.
That's the moment, while it's sliding, the limbs
compressed close to the body, the arms
bent like a crab's rosy legs, the
thighs closely packed plums in heavy syrup, the
legs folded like the white wings of a chicken—
that is the center of life, that moment when the
juiced bluish sphere of the baby is
sliding between the two worlds,
wet, like sex, it *is* sex,
it is my life opening back and back
as you'd strip the reed from the bud, not strip it but
watch it thrust so it peels itself and the
flower is there, severely folded, and
then it begins to open and dry
but by then the moment is over,
they wipe off the grease and wrap the child in a blanket and
hand it to you entirely in this world.

Little Things

After she's gone to camp, in the early
evening I clear Liddy's breakfast dishes
from the rosewood table, and find a small
crystallized pool of maple syrup, the
grains standing there, round, in the night, I
rub it with my fingertip
as if I could read it, this raised dot of
amber sugar, and this time
when I think of my father, I wonder why
I think of my father, of the beautiful blood-red
glass in his hand, or his black hair gleaming like a
broken-open coal. I think I learned to
love the little things about him
because of all the big things
I could not love, no one could, it would be wrong to.
So when I fix on this tiny image of resin
or sweep together with the heel of my hand a
pile of my son's sunburn peels like
insect wings, where I peeled his back the night before camp,
I am doing something I learned early to do, I am
paying attention to small beauties,
whatever I have—as if it were our duty to
find things to love, to bind ourselves to this world.

The Latest Injury

When my son comes home from the weekend trip where he
stood up into a piece of steel in the
ceiling of a car and cut open his head and
had the wound shaved and sprayed
and stitches taken, he comes up to me
grinning with pride and fear and slowly
bows his head, as if to the god of trauma,
and there it is, his scalp blue-grey as the
skin of a corpse, the surface cold and
gelatinous, the long split
straight as if deliberate, the
sutures on either side like terrible
marks of human will. I say
Amazing, I press his head to my stomach
gently, the naked skin on top
quivering like the skin on boiled milk and
bluish as the epidermis of a monkey
drawn out of his mother dead, the
faint growth of fine hair like a
promise. I rock his brain in my arms as I
once rocked his whole body,
delivered, and the wound area glows
grey and translucent as a fledgling's head when it
teeters on the edge of the nest, the cut a
midline down the skull, the flesh
jelly, the stitches black, the slit saying
taken, the thread saying given back.

The Quest

The day my girl is lost for an hour,
the day I think she is gone forever and then I find her,
I sit with her awhile and then I
go to the corner store for orange juice for her
lips, tongue, palate, throat,
stomach, blood, every gold cell of her body.
I joke around with the guy behind the counter, I
walk out into the winter air and
weep. I know he would never hurt her,
never take her body in his hands to
crack it or crush it, would keep her safe and
bring her home to me. Yet there are
those who would. I pass the huge
cockeyed buildings massive as prisons,
charged, loaded, cocked with people,
some who would love to take my girl, to un-
do her, fine strand by fine
strand. These are buildings full of rope,
ironing-boards, sash, wire,
iron-cords woven in black and blue spirals like
umbilici, apartments supplied with
razor-blades and lye. This is my
quest, to know where it is, the evil in the
human heart. As I walk home I
look in face after face for it, I
see the dark beauty, the rage, the
grown-up children of the city she walks as a
child, a raw target. I cannot
see a soul who would do it, I clutch the
jar of juice like a cold heart,

remembering the time my parents tied me to a chair and
would not feed me and I looked up
into their beautiful faces, my stomach a
bright mace, my wrists like birds the
shrike has hung by the throat from barbed wire, I
gazed as deep as I could into their eyes
and all I saw was goodness, I could not get past it.
I rush home with the blood of oranges
pressed to my breast, I cannot get it to her fast enough.

Gabriel and the Water Shortage

When the water shortage comes along
he's been waiting all his life for it,
all nine years for something to need him as the
water needs him now. He becomes
its protector—he stops washing, till dirt
shines on the bones behind his ears
over his brain, and his hands blaze like
dark badges of love. He will not
flush the toilet, putting the life of the
water first, until the bowl
crusts with gold like the heart's riches and his
room stinks, and when I sneak in and
flush he almost weeps, holds his
hands a foot apart in the air and
says do I know there is only about
this much water left! He befriends it, he
sits by its bedside as if it is a dying
friend, a small figure of water
gleaming on the sheets. He keeps a tiny
jar to brush his teeth in, till green
bugs bathe in its scum, but talk about
germs and he's willing to sacrifice his health

to put the life of the water first, its
helplessness breaks his heart, the way it
waits at all the faucets in the city for the
cocks to be turned, and then it cannot
help itself, it has to spill
to the last drop. Weeks go by and
Gabriel's glazed with grime, and every
cell of dirt upon his body is a
molecule of water saved and he
loves those tiny molecules
translucent as his own flesh in the spring, this
thin vivid liquid boy who has
given his heart to water, element
so much like a nine-year-old—you can
cut it, channel it, see through it and
watch it, then, a fifty-foot
tidal wave, approaching your house and
picking up speed as it comes.

Liddy's Orange

The rind lies on the table where Liddy has left it
torn into pieces the size of petals and
curved like petals, rayed out like a
full-blown rose, one touch will make it come apart.
The lining of the rind is wet and chalky as
Devonshire cream, rich as the glaucous
lining of a boiled egg, all that protein
cupped in the ripped shell. And the navel,
torn out carefully,
lies there like a fat gold
bouquet, and the scar of the stem, picked out
with her nails, and still attached to the white
thorn of the central integument,
lies on the careful heap, a tool laid
down at the end of a ceremony.
All here speaks of ceremony,
the sheen of acrid juice, which is all that is
left of the flesh, the pieces lying in
profound order like natural order,
as if this simply happened, the way her
life at 13 looks like something that's just
happening, unless you see her
standing over it, delicately clawing it open.

When My Son Is Sick

When my son is so sick that he falls asleep
in the middle of the day, his small oval
hard head hurting so much he
prefers to let go of consciousness like
someone dangling from a burning rope just
letting go of his life, I sit and
hardly breathe. I think about the
half-liquid skin of his lips,
swollen and nicked with red slits like the
fissures in a volcano crust, down
which you see the fire. Though I am
down the hall from him I see the
quick bellies of his eyeballs jerk
behind the greenish lids, his temples
red and sour with pain, his skin going
pale gold as cold butter and then
turning a little like rancid butter till the
freckles seem to spread, black little
islands of mold, he sleeps the awful
sleep of the sick, his hard-working heart
banging like pipes inside his body, like a
shoe struck on iron bars when
someone wants to be let out, I
sit, I sit very still, I am out at the
rim of the world, the edge they saw
when they knew it was flat—the torn edge,
thick and soil-black, the vessels and

veins and tendons hanging free,
dangling down,
when my boy is sick I sit on the lip of
nothing and hang my legs over
and sometimes let a shoe fall
to give it something.

The Prayer

(for my daughter)

Today I remembered the dryness of her mouth as she
sat in the underground waiting room while her
gerbils were being gassed. It was all she could
say and she said it over and over,
I am thirsty, like a prayer, as he pumped the air
out of the euthanasia box
and pumped the monoxide in, and they curled
up on their sides, her babies, their paws
cupping the blue tumors on their bellies
like hoarded treasure. She sat against the
wall, with just the width of it
between her back and the earth, solid
dirt—and there was still time to save them,
her heart pumping, she was sweating, pallid, not
salivating at all, the adrenaline
rushing through her body to help her burst through the
waiting-room door and rip out the gas-pipe and
scoop them up in her palms while their tails still twitched,
the adrenaline pumping through her body to give her the
strength to stay there in her chair and let the
blue tumors be put to sleep, and she
sat there and said *I'm thirsty, I'm thirsty*.
She did not want to talk about heaven,
she did not want to talk about death,
she did not want to talk about orange juice,
she did not want to talk about thirst,
she just wanted to say it, over and over,
the way you repeat something when you are learning it
for the first time, *I am thirsty. I am thirsty. I am thirsty.*

The Signs

As I stand with the other parents outside the
camp bus, its windows tinted black
so we see our children, if we can find them, as
figures seen through a dark haze, like the dead,
I marvel at how little it takes to
tell me which is Gabriel—just a
tuft of hair, like the crest on the titmouse that
draws the titmice swiftly to its side.
Or all I see is the curve of a chin
scooped and pointed as some shining Italian
utensil for milk-white pasta with garlic,
that's my boy. All the other
mothers, too, can pick their kid by a
finger, a nose in the smoked mirror
as if we have come to identify their bodies
and take them home—such a cloud of fear and longing
hangs above the long drawn-out departure,
but finally it's over, each hand made of
just such genes and no others
waves its characteristic wave,
Gabey's thin finny hand
rotating like a windshield wiper, and they're
off in a Stygian stink of exhaust,
and then I would know his bus anywhere, in
any traffic jam, as it moves through the
bad air with the other buses,
its own smooth black shoulder
above the crowd, and when it turns the corner
I would know this world anywhere
as my son's world, I would love it any time in his name.

I See My Girl

When I see you off to camp, I see you
bending your neck to the weight of your cello, I
see your small torso under the
load of your heavy knapsack the way a
boulder would rest on the body of a child, and
suddenly I see your goodness, the weight of your
patient dogged goodness as you slog your
things to the plane, you look like a small-boned
old lady from darkest Europe
going toward steerage, carrying all the family goods.
Suddenly the whole airport is full of your goodness, your
thin hair looks whittled down by goodness, your
pale face looks drained of blood, your
upward gaze looks like the look of
someone lying under a stone.
For so long I prayed you would be good,
prayed you would not be anything like Hitler as
I as a child feared I was like Hitler—but I
didn't mean this, the oppression of goodness, the
deadness. You ask for something to eat
and my heart leaps up, I take off your backpack and we
lean your cello against a chair and
then I can sit and watch you eat chocolate pudding,
spoonful after careful spoonful, your
tongue moving slowly over the mixture
in deep pleasure, *Oh it's good, Mom,*
it's good, you beam, and the air around your face
shines with the dark divided shining of goodness.

The Green Shirt

For a week after he breaks his elbow
we don't think about giving him a bath,
we think about bones twisted like white
saplings in a tornado, tendons
twined around each other like the snakes on the
healer's caduceus. We think about fractures and
pain, most of the time we think about pain,
and our boy with his pale set face goes
around the house in that green shirt
as if it were his skin, the alligator on it with
wide jaws like the ones pain has
clamped on his elbow, fine joint that
used to be thin and elegant as
something made with Tinkertoy, then it
swelled to a hard black anvil,
softened to a bruised yellow fruit,
finally we could slip the sleeve over,
and by then our boy was smelling like something
taken from the back of the icebox and
put on the back of the stove. So we stripped him and
slipped him into the tub, he looked so
naked without the sling, just a boy

holding his arm with the other hand as you'd
help an old geezer across the street, and
then it hit us, the man and woman by the
side of the tub, the people who had made him,
then the week passed before our eyes
as the grease slid off him—
the smash, the screaming, the fear he had crushed his
growth-joint, the fear as he lost all the
feeling in two fingers, the blood
pooled in ugly uneven streaks
under the skin in his forearm and then he
lost the use of the whole hand,
and they said he would probably sometime be back to normal,
sometime, probably, this boy with the long fingers of a surgeon,
this duck sitting in the water with his L-shaped
purple wing in his other hand.
Our eyes fill, we cannot look at each other,
we watch him carefully and kindly soap the damaged arm,
he was given to us perfect, we had sworn no harm
would come to him.

Gerbil Funeral

By the time we're ready it's dark, so somebody
goes for a flashlight and we all troop out to the grave
by its shuddering light. The beam goes down
into the hole deep, its talcum
sides a soft gold, the autumn has
been so dry. The crickets begin as
Liddy wraps the coffin in black plastic, a
shroud of glittering darkness, and her father with his
long arm sets it in the bottom of the pit.
Then there's a moment of silence, none of us
knows what to do, she takes the shovel and
drops the first spadeful of dirt.
It lands with a crash so the crickets all stop a moment
and she fills it in. She will not let us
help, all that can be done for their bodies
even now her body will do, the
dust flying in a pale net
on her brother holding the light and swaying like the
Second Gravedigger. No one speaks, we
know this girl and the sweat of her silent love.
Five inches from the top, she stops and
waters the shallow pit, kneels and
presses tulip-bulbs into the dirt,

screwing them in like bulbs into sockets,
Black Parrots, Cardinals,
Flaming Parrots, Queens of the Night,
scrapes the rest of the soil in and
waters it again, beginning to flag,
sprinkles grass-seed on the top.
                                  It is over, they are
dead, then, curled in the box with its
scarlet velvet lining, on a bed of
sunflower seeds for the other side,
and where is she? And that love she poured into them,
where is it, now? Dead? She turns and
walks to the house, her heart cold and
hard in her chest as a bulb in the winter ground.

Mouse Elegy

After he petted his mouse awhile,
Gabriel said "He's really still,
he doesn't move at all," running his
small finger over the tiny
luxurious black and white back,
and then in awe and shock he said "He's—
dead." I lifted him out of his cage in his
bed, a brown-rice box, and Gabey
turned and turned his chest as if
struggling to get unstrapped from something,
twisting and twisting from the waist up and then
trying to get ahold of me
several times as if he couldn't, as
if something was holding him by the body but
finally it broke, he came into my arms,
I said whatever you say then,
My darling, my sweetheart.
We got a hanky with roses on it and
laid it on the kitchen floor and laid
Blackie on it. He drifted there like a
long comma,
front paws, pink and tiny as
chips of broken crockery, held
up in wonder, like a shepherd at the Christ Child's
crèche; back paws strong as a jackrabbit's
thrust back in mid-leap; and the
thick whisker of the tail arrested in a
lovely male curve. We kneeled on
either side of the miniature head,

wedge-shaped and white, floating there with an
air of calm absence and demanding dreams.
I started to roll up the hanky, rocking the
light body a little, and one of his
ears unfurled, a grey petal
opening slowly in the night, and then we
wrapped Blackie in red roses and
paper towels, Gabe laid him in the glossy
black box lined with crimson
the champagne came in, we put it in the freezer
until we could take him to the country and crack the
frozen ground with axes so Blackie can
lie with the others in the earth, in a field of mice.

The Month of June: 13½

As my daughter approaches graduation and
puberty at the same time, at her
own calm deliberate serious rate,
she begins to kick up her heels, jazz out her
hands, thrust out her hip-bones, chant
I'm great! I'm great! She feels 8th grade coming
open around her, a chrysalis cracking and
letting her out, it falls behind her and
joins the other husks on the ground,
7th grade, 6th grade, the
purple rind of 5th grade, the
hard jacket of 4th when she had so much pain,
3rd grade, 2nd, the dim cocoon of
1st grade back there somewhere on the path, and
kindergarten like a strip of thumb-suck blanket
taken from the actual blanket they wrapped her in at birth.
The whole school is coming off her shoulders like a
cloak unclasped, and she dances forth in her
jerky sexy child's joke dance of
self, self, her throat tight and a
hard new song coming out of it, while her
two dark eyes shine
above her body like a good mother and a
good father who look down and
love everything their baby does, the way she
lives their love.

Boy Out in the World

Gabriel at ten does not believe in evil,
he judges by himself, he knows no man would
willingly hurt another. He believes in
force, axe against lance, one cross-bow
against two swords, he believes in measurement,
power, division, blood, but not
the malevolent heart, so when he walks home
at 3 o'clock, on West 97th,
down our block past the junkie hotels,
the light burden of his pack on his back
dark-red as some area deep in the body
that is never seen, and the man says to him Hey, kid,
Gabey answers, he meets force with force,
his arms so thin the light comes through the edges, he says
Yeah? And the man asks him a question, so
eager he is for Gabe to explain the world,
the man says You know what *cock* means?
Gabe answers politely and keeps walking,
he feels sorry for a man so dumb he has to ask a
                                    question like that,
and he knows it wasn't a bad man,
he wasn't dressed like a bum or talking like a wino,
and anyway Gabey knows what's what, he can
look deep into his own heart
and tell you the nature of the human—kindness,
courtesy, force.

Life with Sick Kids

One child coughs once
and is sick for eight weeks, then the other child coughs so
hard he nearly vomits, three weeks, and then
stops and then the first child coughs a first cough,
and then the other delicately and dryly begins to cough,
death taking them up and shaking them
as kids shake boxes at Christmas. So in bed on the
third day of the blood when it would be
almost safe to use nothing,
just a tiny door left open for a resourceful child,
I cannot see or feel or smell you, I keep
thinking I hear the unconceived one
cough a little introductory cough.

That Moment

It is almost too long ago to remember—
when I was a woman without children,
a person, really, like a figure standing in a field,
alone, dark against the pale crop.
The children were there, they were shadowy figures
outside the fence, indistinct as
distant blobs of faces at twilight.
I can't remember, anymore,
the moment I turned to take them, my heel
turning on the earth, grinding the heads of the
stalks of grain under my foot, my
body suddenly swinging around as the
flat figure on a weathervane will
swerve when the wind changes. I can't
remember the journey from the center of the field to the edge
or the cracking of the fence like the breaking down of the
borders of the world, or my stepping out of the
ploughed field altogether and
taking them in my arms as you'd take the
whites and yolks of eggs in your arms running
over you glutinous, streaked, slimy,
glazing you I cannot remember that
instant when I gave my life to them
the way someone will suddenly give her life over to God
and I stood with them outside the universe
and then like a god I turned and brought them in.

Looking at Them Asleep

When I come home late at night and go in to kiss the children,
I see my girl with her arm curled around her head,
her face deep in unconsciousness—so
deeply centered she is in her dark self,
her mouth slightly puffed like one sated but
slightly pouted like one who hasn't had enough,
her eyes so closed you would think they have rolled the
iris around to face the back of her head,
the eyeball marble-naked under that
thick satisfied desiring lid,
she lies on her back in abandon and sealed completion,
and the son in his room, oh the son he is sideways in his bed,
one knee up as if he is climbing
sharp stairs up into the night,
and under his thin quivering eyelids you
know his eyes are wide open and
staring and glazed, the blue in them so
anxious and crystally in all this darkness, and his
mouth is open, he is breathing hard from the climb
and panting a bit, his brow is crumpled
and pale, his long fingers curved,
his hand open, and in the center of each hand

the dry dirty boyish palm
resting like a cookie. I look at him in his
quest, the thin muscles of his arms
passionate and tense, I look at her with her
face like the face of a snake who has swallowed a deer,
content, content—and I know if I wake her she'll
smile and turn her face toward me though
half asleep and open her eyes and I
know if I wake him he'll jerk and say Don't and sit
up and stare about him in blue
unrecognition, oh my Lord how I
know these two. When love comes to me and says
What do you know, I say This girl, this boy.

A NOTE ABOUT THE AUTHOR

Sharon Olds was born in 1942, in San Francisco, and educated at
Stanford University and Columbia University. She has been
the recipient of a National Endowment for the Arts grant and
a Guggenheim Foundation Fellowship, and her poems have
appeared in *The New Yorker*, *The Paris Review*, *The Nation*,
Poetry, and other magazines. Her first book of poems,
Satan Says (1980), received the inaugural San Francisco
Poetry Center Award. Her second, *The Dead and the Living*,
was both the Lamont Poetry Selection for 1983 and winner of the
National Book Critics Circle Award. She teaches poetry
workshops at New York University, Columbia University, and
Goldwater Hospital on Roosevelt Island, in New York.

A NOTE ON THE TYPE

This book was set on the Linotype in Janson, a recutting
made direct from type cast from matrices long thought to have
been made by the Dutchman Anton Janson, who was a
practicing type founder in Leipzig during the years 1668–1687.
However, it has been conclusively demonstrated that these types
are actually the work of Nicholas Kis (1650–1702), a
Hungarian, who most probably learned his trade from the
master Dutch type founder Dirk Voskens. The type is
an excellent example of the influential and sturdy Dutch types
that prevailed in England up to the time William Caslon
developed his own incomparable designs from them.

Composed by Heritage Printers, Inc., Charlotte, North Carolina

Printed and bound by Arcata–Halliday Lithographers, Inc.,
West Hanover, Massachusetts

Based on a design by Judith Henry